Plan, Prepare, COOK

Tasty
Drinks and Snacks

Contents

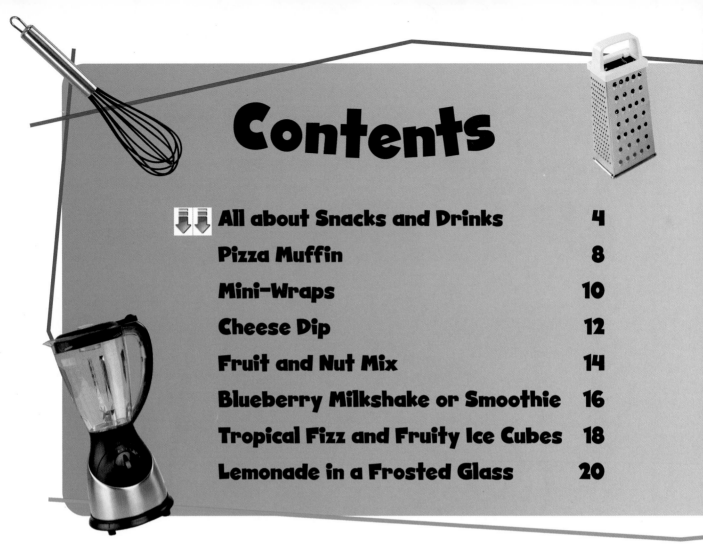

Published by Smart Apple Media,
an imprint of Black Rabbit Books
P.O. Box 3263, Mankato, Minnesota 56002
www.blackrabbitbooks.com

Printed in the United States by Worzalla,
Stevens Point, Wisconsin.
PO1655
4-2014

Published by arrangement with the
Watts Publishing Group LTD, London.

Library of Congress Cataloging-in-Publication Data

Storey, Rita.
 Tasty snacks and drinks / Rita Storey.
    pages cm. -- (Plan, prepare, cook)
 Includes index.

Audience: Grade 4 to 6.
 ISBN 978-1-59920-956-2
 1. Snack foods--Juvenile literature. 2. Beverages--
Juvenile literature. I. Title.
 TX740.S752 2015
 641.5'3--dc23
                                         2013034771

Picture credits
All photographs Tudor Photography, Banbury
unless otherwise stated. Shutterstock p5;
Wishlistimages.co.uk p4

Cover images Tudor Photography
All photos posed by models. Thanks to Jack Abbott,
Amy Mobley, Serish Begum, and Jordan
McElavaine.

Free activity sheets are available for pages marked with ⬇. Request them at info@blackrabbitbooks.com. Find out more on page 32.

Words in **bold** are in the glossary on page 30.

Before You Start

- Wash your hands before and after preparing food.
- Ask an adult to help when the recipe uses the oven or stovetop.
- If you have long hair, clip or tie it back.
- Dry your hands before you plug in or unplug any electrical appliances.
- Wear an apron or an old shirt.
- Wash up as you go along.
- Be extra careful with sharp knives.
- Ask an adult to help with the blender or food processor.
- Ask an adult to help you measure the ingredients.

Look for this useful guide to each recipe.

How long each recipe takes to make.

How difficult each recipe is to make.

Whether the food needs to be cooked.

All about Snacks and Drinks

Snacks and drinks are a useful way of boosting your energy between meals. But eating too many snacks can keep you from being hungry and eating properly at meal times.

Processed Foods

Supermarkets and other stores sell a wide range of foods made in handy sizes to eat as snacks. Many of these **processed foods** are high in sugar and **fat**. Some also have **artificial colorings** and **flavorings** to make them look and taste more attractive. It's best to eat them only occasionally.

Your Diet

What you eat and drink is called your **diet**. There are lots of different foods and drinks to choose from. Try not to eat chips and processed snacks every day. There are lots of healthy snacks that are equally delicious.

The Human Machine

The human body is like a machine that needs **energy** to work. Energy is released from the food you eat and used up by your body. Energy is measured in **joules** or **calories**.

A Healthy Balance

To be healthy, you must eat enough food to produce the energy needed by your body. But if you eat more food than your body actually requires, it is turned into fat.

3

- Sprinkle half of the cheese on top of each muffin.
- **Broil** for 2 minutes or until the cheese has melted and is golden brown.

If You Prefer

Try any of these toppings for a change:

- strips of cooked ham
- chopped, cooked chicken
- slices of zucchini
- pieces of cooked bacon
- pineapple
- pepperoni

Delicious!

10 minutes

Easy

Cooked

Mini-Wraps

These tasty little treats can be stuffed with all sorts of fillings. Experiment with a few different ones! Make up a batch and keep them in the fridge ready for a "snack attack".

Ingredients

- 1 flatbread wrap
- 1 tablespoon cream cheese

Filling of your choice:
- thin slices of ham, chicken salami, cucumber, or tomato

You Will Need

- cutting board
- kitchen knife

If You Prefer

You can use a thin layer of peanut butter instead of cream cheese.

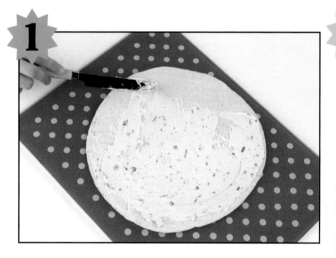

1

- Place the wrap on the chopping board.
- Spread the cream cheese all over the wrap.

2

- Place the slices of meat along the middle of the wrap.

3

- Place the rest of the filling all around the wrap.

4

- Roll into a tight roll.

5

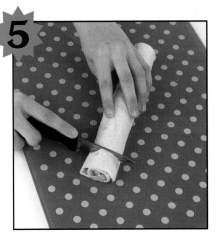

- Cut into bite-sized lengths.

Yum!

Handy Hint

These rolls work best if the filling inside is not too chunky.

10 minutes

Very easy

No cooking

Cheese Dip

This tasty dip makes an ideal snack when you get home from school. Have everything ready in the fridge so that you can eat it right away.

Types of Cheeses

These cheeses have a creamy texture: cream cheese, ricotta, mozzarella

Soft cheese with a soft, sticky texture: Brie, Camembert

Hard cheese that can be grated: Cheddar, Parmesan

You Will Need

- small mixing bowl
- tablespoon
- small serving bowl
- plate

Ingredients

- 4 tablespoons cream cheese
- 2 tablespoons mayonnaise
- 1 tablespoon chopped fresh chives
- sticks of carrot, celery, and cucumber
- breadsticks
- pita bread cut into strips
- tortilla chips

1

- Measure the cream cheese and mayonnaise into a bowl.

2

- Stir until mixed.

3

• Mix in the chopped herbs.

4

• Spoon the mixture into a serving bowl.

5

• Arrange the vegetable sticks, breadsticks, pita bread strips, and tortilla chips around the bowl.

Handy Hint

Remember—if you are sharing the dip with someone else, always break off small pieces and dip those. Never put something into the dip after you have taken a bite out of it.

Get Dipping!

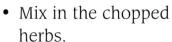

10 minutes

Easy

No cooking

13

Fruit and Nut Mix

Dried fruits and nuts are a filling snack. There are lots of different ones to choose from. Try as many as you can and see which you like, then combine them to make your own special mix.

Dried Fruits

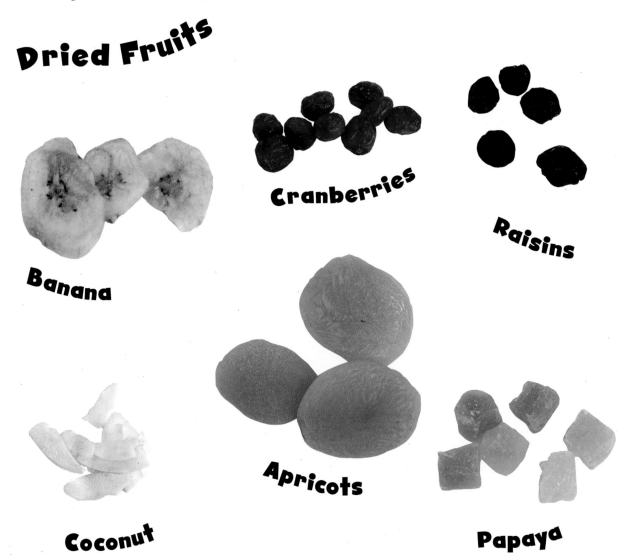

Cranberries

Raisins

Banana

Apricots

Coconut

Papaya

Nuts

Brazil Nuts

Hazelnuts

Pecan Nuts

Walnuts

Handy Hint
Keep some little bags
or containers handy
to fill with a handful
of your special mix.

Almonds

Go Nuts!

| 5 minutes |
| Easy |
| No cooking |

15

Blueberry Milkshake
or Smoothie

A milkshake is made with milk, fruit, and ice cream. A smoothie is made from juice, milk, yogurt, and fruit. Both are equally delicious—take your pick!

Ingredients

Milkshake
- 2 scoops vanilla ice cream
- 1 cup (240 ml) milk
- 1 cup (150 g.) blueberries

Smoothie
- ¾ cup (175 ml) apple juice
- ½ cup (125 ml) plain yogurt
- 1 banana, peeled and sliced
- 1 cup (150 g.) blueberries

You Will Need

Milkshake
- ice cream scoop
- measuring cups
- blender
- glass and drinking straw

Smoothie
- measuring cups
- blender
- glass and drinking straw

Milkshake

1
- Put the ice cream and milk into the blender.

2
- Add the blueberries.

3
- Blend until smooth.

Smoothie

- Measure the apple juice into the blender.

- Add the yogurt, banana, and blueberries.

- Blend until smooth.

Milkshake and Smoothie

- Pour into a glass, add a straw, and enjoy a great-tasting drink.

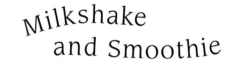

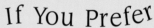

If You Prefer

Strawberries, raspberries, ripe mango, or peach also work well in a milkshake or smoothie.

Mmm!

5 minutes

Easy

No cooking

Tropical Fizz
and Fruity Ice Cubes

This drink is full of **tropical fruit** flavors. Tropical fruits include papayas, mangos, bananas, and pineapples. If you prefer, you can use orange juice instead of tropical fruit juice.

Ingredients

For the Ice Cubes:
- 2 cups (480 ml) water, boiled and left to cool (you can use plain cold water, but boiled water makes the ice cubes very clear)
- small can tropical fruit salad in fruit juice

For the "Fizz":
- 4 cups (960 ml) tropical fruit juice (fresh if possible)
- 1 bottle sparkling water
- a few mint leaves (optional)
- paper umbrellas to decorate (optional)

You Will Need
- measuring cup
- ice cube tray
- strainer
- bowl
- freezer
- glass and drinking straw
- pitcher

1
- Half fill the ice cube tray with the cooled, boiled water.

2
- Rest the strainer on the bowl and pour in the fruit. Leave to drain.

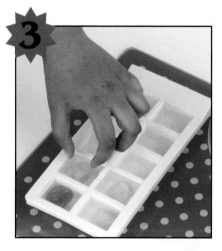

3
- Put a piece of fruit into each ice cube compartment. Freeze overnight until hard.

- When your ice cubes are ready, prepare the "fizz".
- In the pitcher, mix the fruit juice and sparkling water.

- Mix in the rest of the tropical fruit and the fruit juice.

- Remove the ice cubes from the tray.
- Put them in the pitcher and let it get really cold.

Serve the drink with a straw and paper umbrella for decoration.

Fizzylicious!

"Fizz":
5 minutes
Ice cubes:
overnight

Easy

No cooking

Lemonade
in a Frosted Glass

To make this refreshing lemonade extra special, serve it in a pretty, sugar-frosted glass.

You Will Need

- cutting board
- sharp knife
- large pitcher
- tablespoon
- mixing spoon
- glasses
- plate

Ingredients

Per Person
- 1 lemon
- 2 cups (480 ml) water
- 1 tablespoon sugar or honey
- lemon juice and sugar for frosting the glass
- ice cubes (optional)

Citrus Fruits

Lemons, oranges, mandarins, grapefruit, limes, and tangerines are all **citrus fruits**. These fruits contain lots of juice and **vitamin C**. This vitamin is important to keep your body healthy.

1

- Cut the lemon into slices on the cutting board

2

- Put the lemon slices into the pitcher.

3

- Add the sugar.

- Ask an adult to boil some water in a kettle and measure 2 cups (480 ml) into a pitcher.
- Pour the water over the lemons and sugar.

- Stir, then leave in the fridge for a couple of hours until the lemonade is very cold.

- Dip the rim of the glass in lemon juice, then into some sugar.

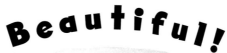

Beautiful!

- Fill the glasses with ice-cold lemonade and enjoy a delicious, refreshing drink.

2 hours

Easy

No cooking

Fruity Yogurt Cone

Try this fruity yogurt to cool you down on a hot day. The added fruit means it is also part of your 5-a-day (see page 6).

(see page 6)

Ingredients

- ice cream cone
- 2 tablespoons fresh fruit, cut into pieces
- 1 scoop store-bought frozen yogurt
- maple syrup or honey
- chopped nuts

Types of Yogurt

Yogurt is made from cow's milk, sheep's milk or goat's milk. The milk is gently heated and thickened to make yogurt.

Natural yogurt does not have anything added to it.

Fruit yogurt has fruit and often sugar added.

Low-fat yogurt has had some of the fat removed from it.

You Will Need

- tablespoon
- ice cream scoop

1
- Put the fruit in the bottom of the cone.

2
- Top with a scoop of frozen yogurt.

3

- Decorate with a small whole fruit or a piece of a larger fruit.

4

- Drizzle a little syrup or honey on the top.

5

- Top with a sprinkle of chopped nuts.

Scrumptious

2 minutes

Easy

No cooking

Hot Chocolate

As an occasional treat on a cold winter's day, this hot chocolate is a wonderful creamy drink.

You Will Need

- small saucepan
- tablespoon
- wooden spoon
- 2 mugs
- tea strainer or small strainer

Ingredients

- 2 tablespoons cocoa powder
- 4 tablespoons sugar
- 4 tablespoons water
- 2 cups (480 ml) milk

To Serve:
- a few mini marshmallows
- a small dish of whipping cream whipped until thick (see page 29)

This serves 2 people.

Milk

Most milk is **pasteurized**. This means that it is heated to destroy any harmful **bacteria**.

Whole milk has nothing added or removed.

2% milk has half of the fat taken out.

Skim milk has most of the fat taken out.

1

- In a saucepan, mix the cocoa powder with one tablespoon of the milk to make a paste.

2

- Stir in the rest of the milk and other ingredients.
- Turn the burner to medium.

3

- Heat the mixture over low heat until the mixture begins to bubble.
- Turn off the burner.

4

- Pour into 2 mugs.

5

- Top with a spoonful of whipped cream.
- Sprinkle on the marshmallows.

6

- Put a small amount of cocoa powder in the tea strainer and shake a little on top of the cream and marshmallows.

Mmmmm

Handy Hint

Be careful not to drink the chocolate until it has cooled a little.

10 minutes

Easy

Cooked

25

Mini Banana Cakes

These easy-to-make, moist cakes are just the thing to give you a boost of energy.

You Will Need

- small saucepan
- wooden spoon
- 3 bowls
- fork
- whisk
- strainer
- mixing spoon
- 2 teaspoons
- cupcake or muffin pan
- cupcake liners
- cooling rack

Ingredients

6 tablespoons butter
2 small, ripe bananas
2 medium eggs
½ cup (125 ml) milk
2 cups (250 g.) self-rising flour
1 teaspoon baking powder
½ teaspoon baking soda
½ cup (115 g.) sugar

Topping:
- caramel sauce and chopped nuts

Before You Start

- Turn the oven on to 375°F (190° C).

1

- Turn the burner on to low.
- Put the butter into the saucepan. Heat until it is melted.
- Turn off the burner.

2

- Mash the bananas with a fork.

3

- Whisk the eggs (see page 29). Add the eggs to the mashed banana.
- Pour on the milk.
- Mix together.

4

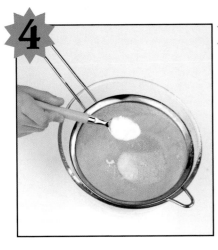

- Sift the flour, baking powder, and baking soda into a bowl.
- Add the sugar.

5

- Add the egg, milk, and banana mixture to the flour mixture.
- Mix them together with a mixing spoon.

6

- Put the cupcake liners into the pan.
- Spoon the mixture into the cupcake liners.
- **Bake** the cakes in the oven for 25 minutes.
- Cool them on a wire rack.

7

- Drizzle on a little caramel sauce and sprinkle with chopped nuts.

Yummmmm

| 50 minutes |
| Medium |
| Cooked |

How To!

Slice

Slicing is preparing something by cutting a thin piece from it. You can slice lots of different foods, including bread, cheese, cucumber, tomatoes, fruits, vegetables, and meat.

- Hold the food firmly. Do not hold too close to the end you are cutting.

- Cut across the food using a sawing action.

Chop

Chopping is cutting something into lots of equal-sized pieces. How small the pieces are depends on what you are cooking. Nuts, fruits, and meat can all be chopped.

- Some things such as nuts need to be chopped very finely. You can do this in a food processor or blender.

- To chop into larger chunks, first take off a thick slice. Cut the slice into pieces first one way, and then the other.

Whisk or Beat

To beat means to stir a mixture quickly to combine everything together.

If the mixture is liquid, you stir it with a whisk.

Beating and whisking add air to a mixture to make it lighter.

Whipping cream is beaten to make it thick.

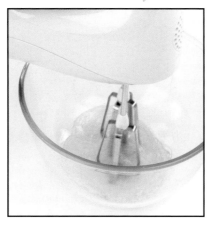

- Beating egg whites is much quicker using an electric mixer.

- If the mixture is liquid, for example eggs, use a fork or whisk.

Grate

A food grater has lots of sharp blades that can turn food into strips.

A box grater has different-sized blades for different foods.

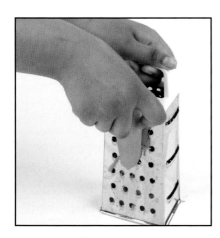

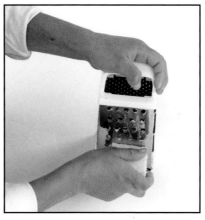

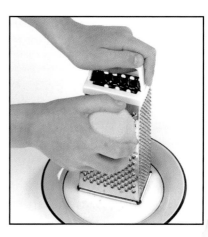

- Cheese and carrots are best grated on the largest blades.

- Hold the top of the grater, press the food against the blades and push down.

- The smallest blades are for grating the rind off oranges and lemons.

Glossary

2% milk Describes a type of milk that has had half of the cream (fat) removed.

artificial coloring A manufactured coloring added to food.

artificial flavoring Manufactured flavors that are added to food.

bacteria Tiny, single-celled micro-organisms.

bake To cook in an oven with heat all around the food.

broil A way of cooking food using direct heat from above or below.

calorie A measurement of the energy in food.

citrus fruit A type of fruit. The best-known citrus fruits are oranges, lemons, grapefruit, and limes.

decay To go bad or rot.

diet The things that you eat and drink.

energy A type of power that can be used. Food is changed to energy in your body.

exercise Physical activity that uses up calories (energy) and improves fitness.

fat 1. A greasy substance found in food. Fats in food are divided into two types: **saturated fats** are found in cream, cheese, butter, fatty meat, and chocolate; **unsaturated fats** are found in avocados, nuts, vegetable oils, and olive oils. Unsaturated fats are healthier than saturated fats. 2. Tissue in the human body where energy is stored.

joule A measurement of energy.

pasteurized Milk that is pasteurized has been heated for a short time to kill any bacteria that could cause food poisoning. Pasteurizing milk also helps it to last longer.

processed food Any food product that has been changed in some way. Cooking, freezing, drying, canning, and preserving are all methods of processing food. Processed foods may contain colorings, flavorings and other additives and preservatives.

protein A substance found in some foods. It is needed by the body to grow and develop properly. Meat, eggs, milk, nuts, and some types of bean contain protein.

savory A taste that is salty or spicy.

skim milk Milk that has had most of the fat removed.

starchy Describes a food that contains starch. Starchy foods make up one of the food groups. They include bread, cereals, rice, pasta, and potatoes.

tropical fruit A fruit grown in a part of the world called the tropics where there are no frosts. Tropical fruits include papayas, mangos, bananas, and pineapples.

vitamin C One of the substances that is essential in very small amounts in the body for normal growth and activity. Vitamin C is found in fresh fruits and vegetables.

whole milk Milk that has nothing added or removed from it.

Equipment

cutting board

tea strainer

strainer

cupcake liners

measuring cup

wire cooling rack

ice cube tray

mixing spoon

whisk

mixing bowl

grater

non-stick saucepan

small sharp knife

kitchen knife

tablespoon

teaspoon

ice cream scoop

You will also need:
dish towel
oven mitts
cupcake pan

wooden spoons

blender

food processor

Index

Activity sheets

Request these free activity sheets at:
info@blackrabbitbooks.com.

Pages 4–5 All about Snacks and Drinks

Plan your snacks and drinks for the week ahead
on this handy food chart. Fill in the shopping list
so you know what you need to buy.

Pages 6–7 All about Snacks and Drinks

What drinks and snack do your friends like best?
Fill in this food survey to find out which are the
most popular.

Page 31 Equipment

Download a colorful poster of all the equipment
used in the *"Plan, Prepare, Cook"* books.